ON THE

STUDY OF MODERN LANGUAGES

IN GENERAL,

AND

OF THE ENGLISH LANGUAGE

IN PARTICULAR

ON THE

STUDY OF MODERN LANGUAGES

IN GENERAL,

AND

OF THE ENGLISH LANGUAGE

IN PARTICULAR.

AN ESSAY,

BY

DAVID ASHER PH. D.

GYAN

Published by

GYAN

Gyan Publishing House
5, Ansari Road
Daryaganj, New Delhi-110002
Phone: 011-47034999, 9811692060
E-mail: books@gyanbooks.com

Distribution Network
gyanbooks.com
India, USA, Canada, UK, Australia

ISBN: 978-81-212-8426-4 (HB)
First Published, 1859

2nd Impression 2024

Printed at: Gyan Press, Delhi.

ON THE STUDY OF MODERN LANGUAGES IN GENERAL, AND OF THE ENGLISH LANGUAGE IN PARTICULAR

Author: DAVID ASHER

ON THE

STUDY OF MODERN LANGUAGES,

ETC.

ON THE

STUDY OF MODERN LANGUAGES

IN GENERAL,

AND

OF THE ENGLISH LANGUAGE

IN PARTICULAR.

AN ESSAY.

BY

DAVID ASHER PH. D.

LONDON:

N. TRÜBNER & CO. 60, PATERNOSTER ROW.

1859.

RECOMMENDATORY NOTICE.

I have read Dr. ASHER's Essay on the Study of the English Language with profit and pleasure, and think it might be usefully reprinted here. It would open out to many English students of their own language some interesting points from which to regard it, and suggest to them works bearing upon it, which otherwise they might not have heard of. Any weakness which it has in respect of the absolute or relative value of English authors does not materially affect its value.

Westminster, July 25. 1859.

RICH[D]. C. TRENCH.

PREFACE.

The flattering reception which has been accorded to the following Essay by the German periodicals to which it was sent for review in its original shape, as the Easter-Programme of the Commercial Academy of Leipsic, and the general desire for a re-issue, openly expressed by the Reviewers, and so cleary manifested by the numerous applications for copies, made to the school and myself, have encouraged me to have the Essay reprinted, permission to do so having been kindly granted me by the Principal of the School. The edition which is now submitted to the public has undergone a careful revisal, and some few additions have been made to the notes. To have met with the approbation of so high an authority as the Very Revd. the Dean of Westminster, augurs favourably for its success, and I avail myself of this opportunity publicly to express my warmest thanks to this distinguished scholar for the extremely kind and ready manner in which he complied with my request, though a complete stranger to him, to bespeak for this little volume the indulgence of the English and American public.

Leipsic, September 1859.

The Author.

CONTENTS.

ERRATA.

Page	7 line 7	. . .	*for* Englisch *read* English.
,,	13 ,, 1	. . .	*for* tho *read* tho'.
,,	17 note	. . . .	*for* treaded *read* treated.
,,	33 line 9	. . .	*for* uso *read* use.
,,	34 ,, 1	. . .	*for* opinious *read* opinions.
,,	35 ,, 16	. . .	*for* procedings *read* proceedings.
,,	37 note 22	. . .	*for* copiouses *read* copiousness.
,,	39 line 26	. . .	*for* auxillary *read* auxiliary.
,,	43 ,, 22	. . .	*for* Cony beare *read* Conybeare.
,,	44 note 39	. . .	*for* recertly *read* recently.
,,	46 line 25	. . .	*for* tho *read* to.

CHAPTER I.

Mit jeder Sprache mehr, die Du erlernst, befreist
Du einen bis daher in Dir gebundenen Geist,
Der jetzo thätig wird mit eigner Denkverbindung,
Dir aufschliesst unbekannt gewesene Weltempfindung.
Ein alter Dichter, der nur dreier Sprachen Gaben
Besessen, rühmte sich, der Seelen drei zu haben.
Und wirklich hätt' in sich alle Menschengeister
Der Geist vereint, der recht wär' aller Sprachen Meister.

Rückert II. 180.

THE ADVANTAGES TO BE DERIVED FROM THE STUDY OF MODERN LANGUAGES.

The study of modern languages has often been regarded in a dubious light, so far, at least, as the discipline and development of the mind are concerned. It has been argued that, after all, let a man's knowledge of languages be ever so extensive, it enables him only to express his ideas in a greater variety, without, however, increasing their stock, and expanding the mind[1]. I trust, I shall succeed,

---

[1] The greatest linguist of our own age, the celebrated Cardinal Mezzofanti was wont to say of himself, 'What am I but an ill-bound dictionary'? We are further told by his biographer, Dr. Russel, that he disparaged his gifts to Card. Wiseman, and once quoted a saying, ascribed to Catharine di Me-

ere I conclude this Essay, in showing the fallacy of this argument, and bringing the reader to a different conviction. Nevertheless, it cannot be denied, that there are here, as everywhere, two sides to the question; that, in short, like all erroneous views this, too, involves a partial truth. For, when, on taking an historical survey of the various nations that flourished in former times, we find that none attained a higher state of culture than the ancient Greeks, and that among them the study of foreign tongues formed no branch of education, but that they confined themselves almost exclusively to the study of their own language, so striking a fact would certainly seem to argue very strongly in favour of those who are opposed to linguistic pursuits[2]. And it must be admitted that it certainly was a great advantage to the Greeks to be able to

---

dici who, on being told that Scaliger knew twenty languages, observed, "that is twenty words for one idea. For my part, I would rather have twenty ideas for one word!" See the Life of Card. Mezzofanti, by C. W. Russel D. D. London, 1858.

[2] "The Greeks had no Grammar prior to the Alexandrian age, for they knew no other language. The Romans reduced their language to theory, in consequence of their studying the Greek. The moderns have modelled their Grammar on the principles of the Latin."

Quoted from my private notes of Prof. Heyse's Lectures on the Philosophy and History of Language, delivered at the Berlin University in 1850. —

devote their attention wholly and exclusively to one language, and that language one of, or perhaps, *the* most copious, flexible, harmonious, sonorous, and plastic, ever spoken by man. Nay, I believe, I may, without fear of contradiction, be so bold as to assert, that in its turn, the language of the Greeks was indebted to this exclusive devotion of the people to the vernacular for that high degree of perfection which it attained; for the law of reciprocal action would, without doubt, operate here, as in every other instance. Again, what the Greek student lost in breadth and extent of knowledge, he gained in depth and intensity, and by how much the advantage outweighed the disadvantage may easily be gathered from a contemplation of the works they have produced, from a survey of a literature which has been the wonder and admiration of all ages, and will for ever continue to stand as a proud monument, testifying to the vastness and profundity of the human mind. Above all, the Greeks remained thoroughly original. They may have borrowed from the East in matters of philosophy ad physical science; but the works of imagination they have produced are entirely the creations of their native genius, pure and unadulterated. Hence, those works will in all ages, like the productions of nature herself, serve as models, and be looked up to as the true and genuine standards of good taste and refinement. Such originality cannot be claimed for the literature of the Romans, the nation occupying the next place in the ancient civilized world. Among them, the Greek language was generally studied, and it is well known that they drew largely from Greek sources; that, in fact, the conquered race became, in all intellectual matters, the masters of their conquerors, who, with but few exceptions, cannot claim a higher rank than that of clever imitators[3]. The same phenomenon may be observed in reviewing the literary history of modern nations. In proportion as the language of a people — the vehicle of their thoughts — becomes an object of attention, or is made a subject of study by the educated classes, and acquires a fixed character and greater refinement, literature will improve and flourish, and react, in its turn, on the language, enriching it and more amply developing its resources, the two, naturally, going hand in hand together, and being closely allied. Thus, for instance, the progress and development of the German language was greatly retarded by the absurd practice, formerly prevalent among the erudite, of writing their works in Latin; nay, the great Prussian king, Leibnitz, our first great philosopher, and subsequently the king of scholars of our own time, Alex. v. Humboldt (tho' the latter only in a few instances) resorted even to

[3] Compare Hor. Epist. II. 1. 156.

the French language, all these writers preferring to render their works accessible tho the scholars of all countries, instead of contributing, like a Dante, a Montaigne, a Milton (I am, of course, alluding to his prose writings), and a Locke, to enrich and fix the character of their native tongue. Just praise has therefore been bestowed on the philosopher Christian Thomasius, who, the first in modern times, employed the German language in his writings, and, thereby, in some degree, popularized philosophy. Luther and the theological writers of his age cannot here be taken into account, however great the merit due to them for the share they had in developing the resources of the vernacular; for it must not be forgotten, that it was not until the German mind became impregnated with the ideas of our great modern philosophers that the second classical period of our literature took its rise, that a Goethe and a Schiller brought their mighty genius to bear upon the language, and for ever fixed its character.

But linguistic studies have since that time acquired a much higher value. Besides affording to us — what indeed has been entirely overlooked in the fallacious argument mentioned above — a key to the literature of other nations, which cannot fail to expand the mind and furnish it with new ideas, the study of languages, as carried on in our days, is, in itself, a mental discipline, and ranks with other scientific pursuits [4]. It is to the labours of the brothers Schlegel, Wilh. v. Humboldt, Jacob and Wilh. Grimm, Bopp, Lassen, and others that we are indebted for the new science of comparative or historical philology which has so considerably raised the dignity of linguistic studies [5]. The different

---

[4] Besides Herrig's ably conducted "Archiv", Wolf and Ebert's "Annual for English and Romance Literature", and the Berlin Society for the Study of Modern Languages, we have now an "Encyclopædia of the Philological Study of Modern Languages, by Dr. B. Schmitz, Greifswalde 1859," a comprehensive volume, chiefly of a bibliographical value. It having only come to hand while this was under the press, I have not yet been able to test its pedagogical merits. The work decidedly indicates progress, and will be hailed with satisfaction by all engaged in the tuition of the English and French languages, to which two it is more exclusively devoted.

[5] J. Grimm in his Essay "On the Origin of Language", to which we shall have occasion to revert in the following chapter, passes an encomium upon the Petersburgh Dictionary, published by command of the Empress Catharine in the years 1787 — 90, as having first given rise to, and furthered the science of comparative philology. See the above Essay in the "Abhandl. d. Kön. Akad. d. Wissenschaften zu Berlin." 1851, p. 105. —

It is here but due to the Danish philologer Erasmus Rask to state that the mutual relation of the Greek and Scandinavian, in their initial consonants was, for the first time, formally announced by him in his "Enquiry into the Origin of the old Northern or Icelandic Language", a work which was published in Danish in 1818, being one year previous to the publication of Grimm's Grammar. In that work, Rask may

languages, both ancient and modern, are no longer, as formerly, in the days of empiricism, studied by themselves, and viewed in their isolated character; but they are treated as connected with one another by the closest family ties, and as descending from one common stock. — Thus we have now a modern philology, and both French and Englisch scholars, the latter more especially, have successfully vied with their German predecessors in reducing the Grammars of their languages to a more scientific system, and in promoting the more accurate etymology of their vocabularies. All this, however, is too familiar to the reader to require being expatiated upon by me. But there is another, still higher, because purely philosophical view of the question, which, I trust, will infallibly ensure conviction, if

be said to have paved the way for Grimm's great discovery of the law of sound- shifting (Lautverschiebung) on which his theory is mainly based. See Blackwood's Edinb. Magaz. vol. XLVII. No. 292. p. 210.

Nor can we omit to mention in this place an interesting discovery made by the London correspondent of the Berlin National Zeitung, who, in a recent letter on the subject, claims for the learned, but unfortunate Eugene Aram, of romantic celebrity, the merit of being the true father of comparative philology, a manuscript copy of a dictionary on the principles of this science having been left by him, and examined by Bucher. Of course, Eugene Aram had no knowledge of Sanscrit, and hence assumes the Celtic language to be the common parent, and the original source from which the English derives. —

any doubt be left on the reader's mind as to the advantages to be derived from the study of modern languages. Among others who have treated the subject, Arthur Schopenhauer, in his remarkable work "Parerga and Paralipomena", has devoted a chapter to this topic, and illustrated it with his usual felicity. I hope, therefore, the reader will bear with me, if I here quote the passage at full length. To the English reader the quotation will, I trust, be the more welcome, no translation of the work having as yet been undertaken.

"The study of several languages", he says, "is not only an indirect, but also a direct and important mental discipline. Hence, the dictum of Charles V, 'By how many languages a man knows, by so much is he multiplied'. The reason is this. Not every word of a language has its exact equivalent in another. Hence, not all ideas, conveyed by the words of one language, are precisely the same as those expressed by another, altho' such is mostly, nay, sometimes even with striking accuracy, the case, as in the instance of σύλληψις and conceptio, Schneider and tailleur; often, however, the ideas implied, tho' similar and cognate, are modified by shades of difference. A few examples may serve to illustrate my meaning.

Ἀπαίδευτος,	rudis,	roh,
ὁρμή,	impetus,	Andrang.
Seccatore,	Quälgeist,	importun,

Ingénieux,	sinnreich,	clever,
Geist,	esprit,	wit,
Witzig,	facetus,	plaisant,
Malice,	Bosheit,	wickedness,

to which a great many others and, doubtless, more striking ones might be added." —

"Sometimes a language is deficient in a word for some particular idea, while such word is found in most, or even in all other, languages: a most scandalous (*sic!*) instance thereof is the deficiency of the French language, as regards the verb '*to stand*'. — Again, for some ideas only *one* language has a word, which is, then, transferred into other languages; such as the Latin 'affectus', the French 'naif', the English 'comfortable', 'disappointment', 'gentleman', and many similar ones. Occasionally, a foreign language expressses some idea with a slight modification, such as our own does not convey, but which just happens to hit our meaning: in that case every one, solicitous about the accurate expression of his thoughts, will be sure to use the foreign word, without caring for the noisy declamation of pedantic purists. In all cases, where, in one language, an idea is not expressed with the same accuracy as in another, the dictionary places several terms in juxta-position to explain the meaning of the word, thereby fixing the boundary line, as it were, within which the idea lies; without, however, hitting it exactly. Thus, for instance, the Latin '*honestus*' is variously rendered or paraphrased by 'honorable, honest, kind, civil, handsome, decent, worshipful, genteel' etc., and in the same manner the Greek *σώφρων* is treated. Hence it is that all translations are necessarily inadequate. Scarcely ever can any characteristic and striking sentence be rendered so as to convey exactly the same sense in another language. — Every translation, therefore, is inanimate, and its style constrained, stiff, and unnatural: or it is free, i. e. contents itself with an *à peu près*, and that is wrong. A library of translations may be fitly compared to a picture-gallery of copies." —

"Accordingly, one of the principal difficulties in acquiring a language is, fully to understand every idea for which it has a word, when there is no equivalent for the same in our own tongue, as, indeed, is often the case. Hence, then, in studying a foreign idiom, new notions find their entrance into the mind, and we *not only acquire new words, but even new ideas* .... Nor can we be said to have seized the genius of a foreign tongue, until we duly comprehend all the ideas implied by the several words of the language we are studying, and until, in using a term, we immediately attach to it the precise idea it is intended to express, without first translating it into our native tongue, and employing it in the sense which it there conveys, but which often is not an exact equivalent. The same rule holds good with regard to whole phrases. But, once having penetrated into the genius of a foreign language, we have made great progress towards an acquaintance with the nation that speaks it; for, as the style characterizes an individual, so does the language characterize a nation. No one, however, can be said to have thoroughly mastered a foreign idiom, unless he be capable of translating into it not only books, but his very self; so that, without any detriment to his individuality, he be able, in a direct manner, to communicate himself in any tongue, and be as intelligible to foreigners as to his own countrymen."

"Men of inferior capacity will not easily acquire a foreign language to perfection; they may, indeed, get hold of the words, but they will be sure to use them as equivalents to those of their native tongue, and employ, moreover, the turns and phrases peculiar to the latter. The fact is, they are unable to seize the genius of any foreign language, simply, because their train of thought is not spontaneous, but, for the most part, engendered by, and borrowed from, the language in daily use with them, and whose current phrases furnish them with ideas. Hence, too, even in the vernacular, they constantly make use of hackneyed phrases, and string them together so awkwardly withal, that it becomes manifest, how imperfectly they comprehend the meaning even of those phrases, and how, parrot-like, they only utter words without reflection. On the contrary, originality of phraseology, and individual appropriateness of expression are infallible symptoms of a superior mind. From all this it is rendered evident that, in studying a foreign language, new ideas are generated, enabling the speaker to attach a meaning to new signs; that conceptions are severed, which formerly were united into one general, and, therefore, vaguer idea, because there was only one word to denote them; that relations, till then unknown, are discovered, the foreign language expressing the idea by a peculiar metaphor: that, therefore, an infinite number of shades of meaning, analogies, differences, and relations of things enter into the mind by means of the newly acquired language, and a more comprehensive view of things in general is gained. Hence it follows that, in every language, the train of thought varies, and, consequently, by acquiring another idiom, our own train of thought becomes modified, and receives a new tincture; and hence is is that the study of foreign languages, besides its great indirect advantages, constitutes a direct discipline of the mind, inasmuch as it rectifies and perfects our views, while, at the same time, it expands and subtilizes our ideas, and gives a more correct shape to our reflections"[6].

[6] Compare also on this topic "F. A. Wolf's Darstellung der Alterthumswissenschaft nach Begriff, Umfang,

I believe, I need not add another word, tho certainly a great deal more might be added, to prove the utility of linguistic pursuits, and to expose the fallacy of the opposite view of the question. Is has been, I trust, satisfactorily shown that, whether as regarded by itself, or as affecting the mind of the student, the sudy of languages — be they ancient or modern, dead or living — may claim equal rank with any other science, and is well calculated to form an important branch of education. My next object is to prove that, of all modern languages, the English offers to the German student

---

Zweck und Werth", Museum der Alterthumswissenschaft, herausgegeben von F. A. Wolf und Th. Buttmann, Berlin 1807. Bd. 1. p. 91 u. 92

"Gedanken von dem Nutzen richtig getriebener Philologie in der Schule, von G. B. Funk." Berlin 1820. 1. Theil. —

"W. v. Humboldt. Abhandl. über d. Entstehen d. grammat. Formen und ihren Einfluss auf die Ideenentwickelung." (Abhandl. d. hist.-philolog. Klasse d. Kön. Acad. d. Wissensch. zu Berlin 1822. 1823,)

"Ueber die Kawi-Sprache auf der Insel Java." Einleit. B. 1. Berlin 1836. p. 74.

"F. L. v. Stollberg, Ueber unsre Sprache." Ges. Werke. Bd. 10. Hamburg 1827. p. 312.

But above all I would recommend teachers to peruse the excellent little volume "On the Study of Words", by R. Ch. Trench, Dean of Westminster, 8th Ed., London 1858, than whom none has more clearly set forth the advantages of such study.

the greatest advantages, and possesses the highest claims to his attention. I shall consider the question in a threefold light, viz, from the *linguistic*, *literary*, and *practical* point of view.

CHAPTER II.

Now gather all our Saxon bards,
Let harps and hearts be strung,
To celebrate the triumphs of
Our own good Saxon tongue;
For stronger far than hosts that march
With battle-flags unfurled,
It goes with Freedom, Thought and Truth,
To rouse and rule the world.

From "The Triumphs of our Language"
by J. G. Lyons.

THE ENGLISH LANGUAGE CONSIDERED FROM A LINGUISTIC POINT OF VIEW.

The Berlin Academy of Science having, in the year 1794, proposed as a prize question, "To establish an ideal standard of a perfect language; to examine the most celebrated ancient and modern tongues of Europe by that standard, and to show, which of these languages approximated most nearly to it", D. Jenisch, an erudite clergyman of that town, obtained the prize, and published his elaborate treatise under the title of "A philosophico-Critical Comparison and Appreciation of Fourteen Ancient and Modern Languages of Europe, being the Greek, Latin, Italian, Spanish, Portuguese,

French, English, German, Dutch, Danish, Swedish, Polish, Russian, and Lithuanian[7]." In what a rude state linguistic studies then were may be gathered from what, to us, must now appear a most curious note (p. 57), where he deems it necessary to justify his classing English among the Germanic languages. Nor is there throughout the whole work any attempt made, of tracing these various languages to their origin, or seeking a common source for their derivation. The light, which broke in upon the minds of his successors in the same path of science, did not even dawn upon the author of that treatise: indeed, not a gleam of scientific investigation pierces the darkness in which the work is enveloped. Nevertheless, as far as it goes, it is not entirely devoid of merit, and, the conclusions he arrived at being identical with our own, it may well serve our present purpose briefly to state them here. — The conditions which he lays down for a perfect language are, 1) Copiousness; 2) Energy of expression; 3) Perspicuity; and 4) Euphony; and, after examining the aforesaid languages by this test, he awards the palm of excellence, in all but the

[7] The German title is as follows: "Philosophisch-kritische Vergleichung und Würdigung von 14 älteren und neueren Sprachen Europen's, namentlich der griechischen" etc. Eine von der Kön. Preuss. Akad. d. Wissensch. gekrönte Preisschrift des Herrn D. Jenisch, Prediger in Berlin. Berlin, Friedr. Maurer, 1796.

last[1], to the English. "In copiousness" he says (ibid. p. 60), "the English surpasses all other

[1] See, however, on this head, "Hugh Blair's Lectures on Rhetoric," vol. I. Lect. 9, and, among more recent writers, a very able paper from the pen of Voigtman of Jena, in Herrig's "Archiv für das Studium der neueren Sprachen und Literaturen", Second Series, vol. 2, 1847. p. 109 ff. Voigtman is of opinion that, down to Sheridan, the English language, at least as regards the pronunciation of the consonants, had been treaded agreeably to nature and the just laws of sound, but that, since Walker, who particularly misunderstood and disfigured the Romance element, a germ of corruption had been introduced and fostered, which still continues — and at present more than ever — to infect the language. A still more recent writer, however, whom I shall have yet more frequent occasion to quote, has, to my mind at least, finally set the matter at rest, and few will venture to question his verdict. I am referring to Harrison (the Rev. Matthew), who, in his instructive work, "The Rise, Progress, and Present Structure of the English Language", London, Longman and Co. 1848, p. 73, pointing out the monosyllabic character of the Saxon element, and the strength thereby conferred on English poetry, complains of Lord Byron for his complimenting other tongues at the expense of his own in the famous stanza of his Don Juan, running thus,

"I love the language, that soft bastard Latin etc.",

and, in commenting upon it, says, "This very stanza alone is sufficient to rescue the English language from the charge His Lordship has endeavored to fix upon it. If it is expressive of harshness in one part, it is equally expressive of gentleness in another. The first five lines are full of liquids, the gentlest of all sounds. The 'gentle liquids gliding', and the repetition

languages", and it derives this advantage, he justly thinks, from the possession of a literature that has been cultivated for centuries, from the intercourse of the English with other nations, from the political condition of the country, from the unrestrained freedom of the press, which it has ever enjoyed, and which roused and fostered a spirit of free enquiry, and called into existence numerous works of every species of literature[2], and, lastly, to the

---

of '*th*' in 'breathe of the sweet south' are soft and beautifully descriptive. The smoothness and softness of the words exactly represent the poet's meaning. When we come to the words 'uncouth' and the two following lines, Lord Byron would have looked in vain to the 'sweet south' for terms so applicable to the purpose which he had in view, as the terms '*harsh*, *northern*, *whistling*, *grunting*, *guttural*, *hiss*, *spit*, and *sputter*' . . . The materials of the English language are abundant for all purposes, and only require a judicious application. It can drop the honeyed words of peace and gentleness, and it can visit with its '*withering*, *scathing*, *burning*, *blasting*, *curse*.'

Compare also "Die Kunst der deutschen Uebersetzung aus neueren Sprachen, von Tycho Mommsen." Leipzig, A. Gumprecht, 1858. p. 24.

[2] "Let my countrymen too reflect", says the learned Harris in his "Hermes" (Philological Enquiries, Part. I. Ch. IV), "that in studying a work upon this subject (he urgently recommends the study of Lowth's Grammar of the English Language), they are not only studying a language in which it becomes them to be knowing, but a language which can boast of as many good books as any among the living or modern langua-

genius of the nation itself, in which are united, — what has never been found united before, and the like of which is not to be met with now — quickness and depth of feeling, fancy and judgment, talent and erudition." In speaking of energetic diction, and the aptitude of the Germanic family of languages for compounding words, Jenisch, by way of illustration, quotes a passage from Thomson's Seasons, beginning with the line,

"Be gracious, heaven! for now laborious man and spring",

to show, how, on the one hand, the German can well cope with the English in compounding words, and yet, on the other hand, to point out a peculiar excellence of the latter [3]. "In the third line of the

---

ges of Europe. The writers, born and educated in a free country, have been left for years to their native freedom. Their pages have been never defiled with an *Index expurgatorius*, nor their genius ever shackled with the terrors of an inquisition." (I quote from the elegant edition of the author's works, published by his son, the Earl of Malmesbury, London 1841, T. Tegg.) On this subject I would also particularly recommend the reader to peruse Milton's celebrated treatise "Aeropagita", where this topic is handled in a most masterly manner.

[3] Compare the equally instructive and interesting volume, 'English, Past and Present.' 5 Lectures, by R. Ch. Trench, & Third Ed., Revised. London, John W. Parker and Son, West Strand, 1856, p. 72.

original", he says, "the poet apostrophizes the sun in these terms,

'And temper all, thou world-reviving sun!'

"This temper", he continues, "belongs, in my opinion, to those numerous Latin words which enrich the language of the Briton, and, for the most part, have that general and comprehensive meaning, peculiar to them in the Latin original. Similar, felicitous Latin-English words of multifarious significations, and, therefore, always difficult to be rendered in German are, 'liberal', 'eminence', 'profusion', 'dejected', 'delusive', 'anticipate', and the like. In closely imitating such bold compounds as 'world-reviving', 'insect-tribes', 'wide-imperial' (which he renders by "Welt-erquickend", "Insektenarten", "Welt-beherrschend"), the German is more happy, and is fully able to cope with the English." "Only, it is a pity", he adds, "that the insufferable repetition of the article will never permit our tongue wholly to acquire the energy of her British sister."

As a second point, that contributes more particulary to the energy of the English, and is peculiar to that language alone, he mentions the absense of gender with reference to inanimate objects. "In this simplicity of gender", he says, "it excels all the languages we have compared in this treatise, and the English alone has ventured to rid itself of that encumbrance of speech; for as such we may well designate the three personal genders of words, that conduce neither to perspicuity nor to energy. But, moreover, by thus discarding gender, the English has gained the advantage of the Prosopopeia, by means of which the poet or orator personifies abstract ideas or gives life to inanimate objects, and, having invested them with a gender, presents them more vividly and impressively to the imagination than in any other language. Read, for instance, the following passage, 'Of law no less can be acknowledged, than that *her* seat is the bosom of God; her voice the harmony of the world. All things in heaven and earth do *her* homage; the very least as feeling *her* care, and the greatest as not excepted from *her* power.' It is evident that, in German, where the unavoidable article clings to every word, and always requires the corresponding gender to be expressed, this personification cannot be rendered so effective, while, to the English ear, the indication of gender is novel and striking."

As he proceeds in his investigation, he further points out, how both energy and perspicuity are promoted by a construction that is thoroughly free, or rather in exact correspondence with the natural train of thought. For illustration's sake, he quotes the following passage from Ferguson's History of Civil Life.

"Without entering any further on questions either in moral or physical subjects, relating to the manner or to the origin of our knowledge; without any disparagement to that subtility, which would analyze every sentiment, and trace every modus of being to its source; it may be safely affirmed, that the character of man as he now exists, that the laws of his animal and intellectual system, on which his happiness now depends, deserve our principal study"; and he remarks on it, how, by the sparing use of the article, by the easy turn of the participial construction, and by the natural sequence of ideas, those which are logically coherent are so presented to the mind by means of the language here used. And he returns to this topic in a subsequent section, where he compares the Germanic languages with reference to their perspicuity, a quality which, in his opinion, is more especially enhanced by a construction, such as we have described it in his own words above, and not less so by grammatical simplicity. In this last respect the English language is extolled beyond all others. With what degree of justice, the reader will presently be enabled to judge from Jenisch's own illustrations, as well as from what I shall bring forward from other sources, and as the result of my own observations. I proceed with Jenisch. He quotes the sentence "Man was made for society", to point out, how definite, clear, and energetic it is, as contrasted with the German, where two cumbrous articles are required, and bestows due praise on the total absence of any inflection of the article, to indicate case or number. In the use of the definite article, or rather in its proper omission, where the sense of the noun is not limited or determined, he justly sees an excellence which, in this particular, renders the English language superior even to the Greek, "the most perfect speech ever spoken by man"; for even there the article is frequently used without conferring any additional weight on the noun it accompanies. Again, "in the conjugation of the verb", says our author, "the English language has an advantage over the German in its double future or its two auxiliaries, "shall and will."[4] —

[4] The following passage from the "Rambler", as quoted in Lloyd's English Grammar p. 223., may serve to illustrate the variety and precision, which the use of these auxiliaries gives to the language. A Greenland lover, taking leave of his mistress has this speech put into his mouth by Dr. S. Johnson. "I *will* chase the deer, I *will* subdue the whale, resistless as the frost of darkness, and unwearied as the summer sun. In a few weeks I *shall* return, prosperous and wealthy, then *shall* the roe-fish and the porpoise feast thy kindred, the fox and the hare *shall* cover thy couch, the tough hide of the seal *shall* shelter thee from cold, and the fat of the whale *shall* illuminate thy dwelling." It cannot, however, be denied that the right use of these auxiliaries is one of those niceties of language which present an almost insuperable difficulty to all but natives of England. Jenisch himself, it is evident from his explanation in this passage, had not only not mastered the difficulty, but laboured even under a very grave misapprehension on the point in question. — A very learned little

"If", he proceeds, "the English is poorer in conjunctive particles, than either the Greek or the German, it abounds, by way of compensation, in Interjections, expressive of disapprobation, contemptuous rejection, scorn, and the like, such as 'pshaw! fugh!' and many others for which the German, at least, the more refined language, offers no equivalent." Such, then, were the results of a diligent, candid, and impartial enquiry, at a period, when the student was as yet destitute of any landmark to guide him through those vast tracts of uncultivated territory which he was bent on exploring, where no pioneers had preceded him, whose foot-prints the wanderer might have traced and pursued, nay, where no human being had scarcely ever set his foot.[5]

---

volume on the subject, entitled "Shall" und "Will", Two Chapters on Future Auxiliary Verbs: etc. etc. by the Right Hon. Sir Edmund W. Head, Bart. 2. Edition. London, John Murray, 1858, may be consulted with advantage.

[5] It is true, Addison in the 'Spectator', Bishop Lowth in his 'Grammar', and Hugh Blair in his 'Lectures on Rhetoric and Belles Lettres', all of which are works of a prior date than Jenisch's, have severally examined the merits of the English language, and the latter has even pointed out precisely the same excellences that struck Jenisch; but altho' the celebrated 'Lectures' were published at Bâsle, as early as 1788, it does not appear that he was acquainted with them: otherwise, so conscientious an enquirer as Jenisch seems to have been would scarcely have failed to state his source. Besides, altho' they

No wonder, therefore, the Berlin Academy, as Jenisch informs us in his preface, had twice successively to propose the question, ere any one could be found who would venture to handle it. Indeed, in comparing the then state of philology (we mean, of course, comparative philology) with the present, some remarks that once fell from the lips of Macaulay in speaking of shallow knowledge may not inappropriately be applied on this occasion.

"When we talk of deep and shallow", said the great historian, "are we comparing human knowledge with the vast mass of truth which is knowable, and which probably in the course of ages, the human mind will attain to? If that be the meaning, then we are all shallow together, and the greatest men that have ever lived, would be the first to confess their shallowness. What would be the chemists of 1746, or the geologists of 1746, compared with the chemists or geologists of 1846? That various knowledge which entitled Strabo to be called a profound geographer, would now be called ignorance on the part of a girl from the boarding school."[6] The

coincide exactly in their appreciation of the language, of the two, Jenisch took a far wider range and an ampler survey of other languages than Blair, who, to all appearances, was deficient in the primary requisite for such an investigation — a knowledge of the Teutonic tongues. We shall however return to him in the sequel. —

[6] From the Address of Baron (then Mr.) Macaulay, delivered in 1846, at the Edinburgh Philosophical Institution.

same, I maintain, may be said of the linguists of Jenisch's time, as compared with those of the present day. Nevertheless, his labours still have a certain value, and are not entirely destitute of merit. And it is for this reason that I have availed myself of them, and placed the result of his researches before the reader, whom I shall now afford an opportunity of examining, how far the observations of Jenisch are borne out and corroborated by the results of more recent enquiries. I resort, at once, to the highest authority, to him who, above all others, may be designated as the creator of the new science of comparative or historical philology — to Jacob Grimm himself. In his highly interesting Essay "On the Origin of Language", embodied in the Transactions of the Berlin Academy of Science, and also published separately, we meet with the following remarkable passage. "Among all modern languages there is not one that, by discarding and upsetting the laws of sound, and by dropping nearly all inflections, has gained greater vigour and force than the English, which, moreover, from an abundance of free medials (Mitteltöne) — which cannot indeed be taught, but may be acquired — derives an energy of expression, such as perhaps no human tongue could ever command.[7]

[7] For the subsequent portion of the quotation I have taken the liberty of adopting Trench's rendering, who, I am happy

Its highly spiritual genius, and wonderfully happy development and condition, have been the result of a surprisingly intimate union of the two noblest languages in modern Europe, the Teutonic and the Romance. — It is well known in what relation these two stand to one another in the English tongue; the former supplying in far larger proportion the material groundwork, the latter the spiritual conceptions. In truth the English language, which by no mere accident has produced and upborne the greatest and most predominant poet of modern times, as distinguished from the ancient classical poetry (I can, of course, only mean Shakspeare), may with all right be called a world-language; and like the English people appears destined hereafter to prevail with a sway more extensive even than its present over all the portions of the globe. For in wealth, good sense, and closeness of structure no other of the languages at this day spoken deserves to be compared with it — not even our German, which is torn, even as we are torn, and must first rid itself of many defects, before it can enter boldly into the lists, as a competitor with the English." Such words, emanating from so eminent a scholar and so ardent a patriot, will, undoubtedly, have due weight with every reader and infallibly ensure

---

to find, has availed himself of the same authority in support of his opinion. See his "English, Past and Present", p. 36.

conviction on the question in every candid mind. All that is left for me now to do is, to amplify what Grimm has only lightly touched, and by entering more minutely into the subject, and by more closely examining the English language, to confirm — if, indeed, confirmation were any longer needed — all that the great philologer has stated. —

Our attention, naturally, is first directed to the origin of the language under examination, and for this purpose, I shall take a brief survey of its history, and give a rapid sketch of its development. The elements, then, of which the language is composed are, the Celtic, the Anglo-Saxon, the Danish, and the Anglo-Norman (including a number of words immediately derived from the Latin), to which must be added several of miscellaneous descent.[8] To show the numerical proportion which these various elements bear to each other I will quote Latham[9], who says, "Let the present language of England (for illustration's sake only) consist of 40,000 words. Of these let 30,000 be Anglo-Saxon, 5000 Anglo-Norman, 100 Celtic, 10 Latin of the

---

[8] For a curious hypothesis on the Tartaric origin of English I would refer the reader to Harrison, as above, p. 6.

[9] "The English Language." By R. G. Latham, M. D. F. R. S. Third Ed. London, Taylor, Walton, and Maberley. 1850. p. 111.

Compare also Phil. Châsles, "Études sur la littérature et les moeurs de l'Angleterre au XIXe Siècle." Paris 1850.

first, 20 Latin of the second, and 30 Latin of the third period, 50 Scandinavian, and the rest miscellaneous." The immense preponderance of the Anglo-Saxon or Germanic element is thus, at once, rendered manifest. But it may not be uninteresting to exhibit, at the same time, to what extent that element prevails over the Anglo-Norman in some of the principal authors. I resort for this purpose to Sharon Turner, who has extracted passages from 15 different authors, and had the Saxon words printed in Italics, to distinguish them from the Anglo-Norman. From these extracts it appears that we have

in the Translat. ,, of the Bible,	125	of Saxon origin	out of	130	words,
,, Spenser, . . .	58	,, ,, ,,	,, ,,	72	,,
,, Shakspeare, .	68	,, ,, ,,	,, ,,	81	,,
,, Cowley, . . .	56	,, ,, ,,	,, ,,	66	,,
,, Milton, . . .	74	,, ,, ,,	,, ,,	90	,,
,, Swift, ...	77	,, ,, ,,	,, ,,	87	,,
,, Addison, . .	64	,, ,, ,,	,, ,,	79	,,
,, Locke, ...	74	,, ,, ,,	,, ,,	94	,,
,, Pope, ...	56	,, ,, ,,	,, ,,	84	,,
,, Young, . . .	75	,, ,, ,,	,, ,,	96	,,
,, Thomson, . .	64	,, ,, ,,	,, ,,	78	,,

In the 4 following authors, Robertson, Hume, Gibbon, and Johnson[10] (well known as the writers

[10] On the variety of composition which the English admits of, Harrison remarks, "In this respect, Swift and

of Latinized diction), the two elements are not only more equally distributed, but the balance is rather in favour of the Anglo-Norman.[11]

Johnson may be considered as placed at opposite extremes: the style of the former being peculiarly *English;* that of the latter being formed upon the classical models, and imitating not only the phraseology, but the polish and rotundity of their periods. Swift would say, 'The thing has not life enough in it, to keep it sweet.' — Johnson, 'The creature possesses not vitality sufficient to preserve it from putrefaction.' How widely different is the phraseology of these sentences! yet they both express the same meaning, and we call them both English." He advises, however, a judicious admixture of A. S. and classical terms. —

[11] Sharon Turner adds, "From the preceding instances we may form an idea of the power of the Saxon language, but by no means a just idea; for we must not conclude that the words which are not Saxon could not be supplied by Saxon words. On the contrary, Saxon terms might be substituted for almost all the words not marked as Saxon." (See his 'History of the Anglo-Saxons from the earliest period to the Norman conquest.' vol. II. Paris, Baudry's European Library, p. 275). I must, however, remark that his etymology, in some instances, is liable to doubt, and that he is not always guided by fixed principles in tracing the origin of words. Thus, for instance, he regards "try" and "stay" as of A. N., but "time" and "mind" as of A. S. derivation. Again, in those lists or tables, where he exhibits the affinities of A. S. with the Latin, Greek, Hebrew, Sanscrit, Chinese, and numerous other languages of all parts of the world, his conjectures are frequently most arbitrary and fanciful, tho', occasionally, it must be admitted, very ingenious.

To continue the analysis down to our own day, I will add two specimens taken from Macaulay and Carlyle, and adopt Sharon Turner's mode of distinguishing the Saxon from the Norman words.

"*The* events *which I* propose *to* relate form *only a* single act *of a great* and event*ful* drama extending *through* ages, *and must be very* imperfectly *understood unless the* plot *of the* preceding acts *be well known. I shall therefore* introduce *my* narrative *by a slight* sketch *of the* history *of our* country *from the earliest* times. — *I shall* pass *very* rapidly *over many* centuries; *but I shall dwell at some length on the* vicissitudes *of that* contest *which the* administration *of king James the* Second *brought to a* decisive crisis."[12]

"*How such* Ideals *do* realise *themselves; and grow wondrously, from amid the* incongruous *ever* fluctuating chaos *of the* Actual; *this is what World-* History, *if it teach any thing, has to teach us. How they grow; and, after long stormy growth, bloom out* mature, supreme; *then quickly (for the blossom is* brief) *fall into* decay; *sorrowfully dwindle; and crumble down, or rush down,* noi*sily or* noise*lessly* disappearing."[13]

---

[12] From Macaulay's History of England, vol. I. p. 3. Tauchnitz Ed.

[13] From Carlyle's French Revolution, vol. I. p. 14. Tauchnitz Ed. — Tennyson's last production, "Idylls of the King",

In point of time, the following is the order of succession in which the various elements composing the language were introduced into it. The first language of the ancient Britons was the Celtic. The Roman occupation, which lasted from 60 b. C. till 410 of the common era, passed without any influence on that language. But, from the period of the Saxon invasion (449), the Celtic was almost entirely superseded by the language of the invaders which was thenceforth called Anglo-Saxon, in contra-distinction from its sister-dialect on the continent, which originally used to be called Dano-Saxon, and now goes by the appellation of Old Saxon. The principal monument of the latter dialect is the *Heliand*[14], while the poem of *Beowulf*, and the *Paraphrases* of Caedmon, the Monk of Whitby († 680) are the chief representatives of the Anglo-Saxon[15]. — In the first half of the eleventh century the Danish element was blended with the Anglo-Saxon, tho' not to any considerable extent, as may be seen from the above enumeration. In

---

is said to be a most remarkable specimen of Saxon English. (See Edinb. Rev. July 1859.)

[14] "Heliand, oder die altsächsische Evangelien-Harmonie." Edited by J. Andreas Schmeller. Munich 1830.

[15] "The Anglo-Saxon Poem of Beowulf etc." Edited by John M. Kemble. London 1833. Second. Ed. 1835.

"Caedmon's Metrical Paraphrase of Parts of the Holy Scriptures etc." Ed. by B. Thorpe. London 1832.

the year 1150 [16] the Anglo-Saxon began to be transformed: not, however, as an effect of the Norman invasion, for the change, as yet, was one rather of form than of matter. The process it underwent is thus stated by Hallam, "The Anglo-Saxon was converted into English, 1. by contracting or modifying the pronunciation or orthography of words; 2. by dropping many inflections, especially of the noun, and consequently making a larger uso of articles and auxiliaries; 3. by the introduction of French derivatives; and 4. by using less inversion and ellipsis in poetical diction. — The language thus transformed, and in use up to 1250, is now generally known by the name of Semi-Saxon, and Layamon (1180), the translator of Wace's *Chronicle of the Brut,* may be named as the principal writer of the period [17]. Philologers, however, differ in

---

[16] The *Saxon Chronicle,* containing an account of the English annals from A. D. 1, and continued by a succession of writers, came to an abrupt conclusion in the year mentioned above.

[17] "Layamon's Translation of Wace's Chronicle of the Brut, with an English Translation etc. Ed. by Fr. Madden, 1847." — For more ample literary notices I can refer the German reader to Dr. Behnsch's "Geschichte der englischen Sprache und Literatur." Breslau 1853. Cf. also "Outlines of Engl. Liter., by T. B. Shaw. London 1849", where a sketch of the history of the Engl. Language is given, of which I have partly availed myself.

their opinious as to the English of this writer, some (such as Ellis and others) considering it as a simple and unmixed, tho' very barbarous Saxon, others (among them Campbell), as the first dawning of English. The last monument of the Semi-Saxon period is supposed to be the *Ormulum*, a metrical paraphrase of the gospel-history, consisting of upwards of 20000 lines in blank verse, whose author was Orm[18]. But already the Norman element had begun to prevail to some extent. Indeed, the contact of the Anglo-Saxons with the French race dates even prior to the conquest (1066). Their sons were partly educated in France. Their sovereigns were related either by the ties of consanguinity or of matrimony. "*Jacke woud be a gentilman, if he coud bot speke Frenshe*", such was the taunt which the pure Anglo-Saxon flung at the imitators of outlandish fashions. It was, however, more particularly at court, where the French language was spoken. Thus, Henry II. (1154) did not even understand his subjects at Pembrokeshire, when they began their address by the simple words, "*Good*

[18] "The Ormulum, now first edited etc. by R. M. White D. D., Oxford 1852." I may here mention that, in the Einladungsschriften zur Prüfung in der Oeffentlichen Handelslehranstalt, 1853 & 1854, my friend and colleague, C. H. Monicke Esq., published, under the modest title of "Notes and Queries on the Ormulum", a highly valuable essay which would well deserve a reprint.

olde kynge." But, as we approach the end of the thirteenth, and advance into the fourteenth century, we find French words imported in masses into the Anglo-Saxon, and, thus, the Norman element more and more extensively amalgamating with it. — Here, then, we are arrived at the period of Old English, which extends from about 1250 down to the age of Chaucer[19]. — Edward III. (1327—1377) had some share in furthering the progress of English among his subjects, for it was he who, in 1362, prohibited the use of French in judicial pleadings, and ordered the English to be substituted in its stead[20]. Wicliffe[21] popularised both religion and the new language by his version of the New Testament, which he completed in the year 1380. From that year parliamentary procedings were also carried on in English, tho' French continued to be the language

[19] "Then", says Macaulay, speaking of the thirteenth century, "was formed that language, less musical indeed than the languages of the south, but in force, in richness, in aptitude for all the highest purposes of the poet, the philosopher, and the orator, inferior to the tongue of Greece alone." (See Hist. of Engl. Tauchnitz Ed. vol. I. p. 17.)

[20] Many words of that period continue, to this day, to be heard in the mouth of the lower classes, and are skilfully reproduced in some of Mrs. Gaskel's novels. Cf. also Harrison, as above, p. 32.

[21] For particulars about the various writers here mentioned I may again refer the reader to Behnsch and Shaw, as above,

of the Upper House down to 1483. Henry V. (1413—1422) strongly recommended his subjects the use of English, and he, as well as his predecessor Henry IV. († 1413), wrote his will in the vernacular. Old English had by this time shifted into what is now termed Middle-English, which dates from Mandeville (about 1350), the father of English prose, and Chaucer († 1400), the father of English poetry. "The last characteristic of a grammar different from that of the present English", says Latham, in mentioning these authors, "is the plural form in — en; we sellen, ye sellen, they sellen. As this disappears, which it does in the reign of Queen Elisabeth (Spenser, † 1599, has it continually), the Middle-English may be said to pass into the *New* or *Modern English.*" This, then, is the language which Shakspeare has rendered immortal by his imperishable works, and which, with comparatively but slight modifications, has continued to be in use ever since. —

Having thus cursorily reviewed the history, and given an analysis of the component elements of the language, I shall now proceed briefly to consider its excellencies, such as they are pointed out and extolled by Grimm. First, as to its copiousness. — On this head but little need be added by me to Jenisch's panegyric, as quoted above. It is evident that an idiom, combining two such rich languages as the Norman (or French) and

Saxon [22] (or German), must necessarily surpass them both, singly, in copiousness, considering that, in so many instances, it has, at least, two words (one of Norman and one of Saxon derivation) for every idea, besides the synonymous terms of purely Norman or Latin [23] origin, or of both stocks together. Thus, to give but one instance, Greenwood [24] enumerates thirty words of mixed descent to express the varieties of the passion of anger. They are, "Anger, wrath, passion, rage, fury, outrage, fierceness, sharpness, animosity, choler, resentment, heat, heart-burning; to fume, fret, chafe, storm, inflame, to be incensed; to vex, kindle, irritate, enrage, exasperate, provoke; to be sullen, hasty, hot, rough, sour, peevish", etc. But, even at the risk of incurring the charge of repetition, how can I refrain from adding my tribute of admiration, when I reflect on the unbounded copiousness of a language which, from that happy mixture of two elements, has to dread nothing from purists, declaiming against the importation of foreign words, [25] and is so admirably adapted to draw its nourishment from all sources, and assimilate it without any detriment

---

[22] On the copiousess of the Anglo-Saxon, compare Sharon Turner, as above, Vol. II. p. 275.

[23] As to the words immediately derived from the Latin, see Trench's Engl. Past and Present, p. 47.

[24] In the Preface to his Grammar.

[25] Compare Trench, as above, p. 105—7, and passim.

to its well-organized body? A language which has been enriched and modelled and ennobled by a Chaucer, a Spenser, a Shakspeare, a Milton, a Dryden, a Pope, a Swift, an Addison, a Gibbon, a Byron, a Shelley, a Scott, a Bulwer, a Dickens, a Thackeray, a Macaulay, and a host of writers of more or less celebrity; which has sustained, and has been rendered more pliable by, the eloquence of a Chatham, a Burke, a Fox, a Sheridan, a Pitt, a Grattan, an Erskine, and a Brougham; which, for centuries, has been listened to in a free senate, has eloquently pleaded at the bar, and has graced the pulpit; which has had, for centuries, a free vent in an unshackled press, has kindled patriotism, has taught kings how to rule, ministers how to govern, and nations how to obey; which has emigrated with an enterprizing people, and, traversing oceans, has aided in civilizing the remotest corners of the world; which has been brought in contact with the far East and the remotest West; to which a commerce, navigation, and the labours of engineering science, such as the world has never witnessed before, have been as tributary streams, deposing their golden sands in its lap, there to be preserved for all times? Can we, then, wonder that a language so constituted, and blessed with such inexhaustible sources of supply, has never yet been locked fast, as it were, and circumscribed within the bounds of a national Dictionary, fixing its limits, and being adopted as a standard by the nation; that all the schemes ever projected for hemming it in within the limits or rather covers of a Dictionary, on the model of the Dictionnaire de l'Académie Française, have, hitherto at least, proved abortive? —

The next excellencies of the English language pointed out by Grimm are its rationality and conciseness of structure. We find these advantages as highly extolled by Blair[26] as by Jenisch. "The English tongue", says the former, "possesses, undoubtedly, this property of being the most simple in its form and construction of all the European dialects. It is free from all intricacy of cases, declensions, moods, and tenses. Its words are subject to fewer variations form their original from than those of any other language. Its substantives have no distinction of gender, except what nature has made, and but one variation in case. Its adjectives admit of no change at all, except what expresses the degree of comparison. Its verb, instead of running through all the varieties of ancient conjugation, suffers no more than four or five changes in termination. By the help of a few prepositions and auxillary verbs, all the purposes of significancy in meaning are accomplished; while the words, for the most part, preserve their form unchanged." The same author, however, takes a wrong view of the

---

[26] Lect. IX. vol. 1.

matter when he speaks of "disadvantages in point of elegance, brevity, and force, which follow from this structure of the language." The contrary has already been shown, and, I trust, satisfactorily, in the earlier portion of this chapter. — Without entering into further details of English grammar, my space being limited, I will simply add that not only is the rationality of English exhibited in these several advantages dwelt on by Blair, but every grammatical rule partakes of the same characteristic. — There is no arbitrariness in any one instance. The language acknowledges no law, but the law of reason and good sense. Hence, too, there is no absurdity to be met with in English grammar, such as — but no, I will not institute comparisons, these being proverbially odious, and perhaps nowhere more so than here, where they touch national sensibility without benefiting science. Suffice it to say that, in every instance, the English language appeals to the understanding, and leaves the decision to reason. — Hence, the study of English grammar proves a most useful discipline of the mind, exercising, as it does, its higher faculties, and not merely memory. Hence, too, tho' it is perhaps the easiest of all grammars, it is yet not without its great difficulties to a dull comprehension, nor without great utility to one of brighter intellect, for it evokes reflection, and brings the reason ing faculty of the individual into play. — No mere reference to even the best English grammar will assist the student in his embarrassment as to placing or omitting the article, — be it the definite or indefinite —; or as to the position of the adverb; or the use of shall and will or should and would; or can and may; or the imperfect or perfect tense; or some and any; — those great stumbling-blocks to the foreigner: but, in all these instances, he will have to consult his own judgment, and to be guided by its decision, provided, of course, he have mastered the genius of the language and its laws, founded still on sound sense alone.

As to the Syntax, it is true that, on opening Lindley Murray[27], we find it to consist of 22 rules — certainly not a formidable number, but my scholastic experience has taught me that, as regards the German student, even that small number might be considerably reduced, nay, that, for him, the whole of the Syntax of the foreign idiom as differing from his own, mainly turns upon the one rule, at once

[27] I quote him, because for a long time his was regarded as the standard Grammar in England, and his name, to this day, is proverbially made the representative of Grammar. Others, however, have long since superseded him, and the most elaborate performance is again, singularly enough, that of an American. I mean of course G. Brown's "Grammar of Engl. Grammars". For a critical summary of Engl. Grams. I can refer the reader to Herrig's Archiv. Vol. XXIII. Part. 3 and 4., p. 406., and to Schmitz's Encycl. p. 106.

simple and natural, which regulates the construction of the sentence in accordance with the sequence of ideas, and, with but few exceptions, requires the Nominative case to precede the verb, and the Objective case to succeed it. Besides this, there are certainly many rules to be observed, such as, the distinction of the habitual from the progressive action, (the latter being expressed by the periphrastic form); the variable position of the negative adverb, according as the answer is expected to be in the affirmative or the negative; the rule of using the plural after 'and', and the singular after 'or'; the preference given, for brevity's sake, to the participial construction; the use of the Accusative with the Infinitive, together with the afore-mentioned niceties and some similar ones: but these I consider to be the peculiar niceties of the language, conferring on it that precision for which it is so eminently distinguished. In whatever light, then, we regard the English tongue, whether by itself or in connexion with its sister-dialects, no one will deny that it deserves a high rank among the branches of study to be pursued by those who aspire to be classed among the well-educated of all countries, no less than by the natives of England themselves. — In concluding this Chapter I can not forbear quoting one more passage from the Review of Grimm's Grammar in Blackwood[28], where

[28] See above, p. 7.

the English are exhorted to "give to comparative philology the honour which it deserves, and which it more especially claims at their hands." "Our native tongue", says the Reviewer, "is nearly, if not altogether, the noblest language that human wisdom, or let us rather say Divine goodness, has ever instituted for the use of man. — It is as nobly descended as it is happily composed. It is united by many links of connexion to the richest and fairest forms of speech in other ages and nations; and it ought to be a primary object of interest among us to study, in all their expansions, its affinities to those sources of copiousness and beauty which have made it what it is . . . If any nation is called to these studies, both by duty and by opportunity, it is ourselves." He then complains of the little that has been done by the English in the peculiar department of comparative philology. This complaint was made in the year 1840. Since then, matters have greatly improved in this respect, and not only have eminent scholars, such as B. Thorpe, Th. Wright, J. M. Kemble, Cony beare, and others, bestowed their labours on the elucidation of the Anglo-Saxon period, editing and translating the more valuable treasures left us of the literature of that language — the parent of English, and writing its history; but all the other elements composing it have been carefully examined, and the valuable contributions of Grimm and other German philologers to the illustration of English have been consulted and called in aid, so that "The English Language" by Latham may now claim a rank, tho' still but a secondary rank, by the side of Grimm's Teutonic Grammar, which first gave the impulse to these studies[29]. —

---

[29] The "Transactions of the Philological Society", of which a number (Part I, 1858) has recertly been published by A. Asher & Co., Berlin, give evidence of the unwearied labours of the members in that direction. Indeed, the very existence of a Society, formed for the investigation of the Structure, the Affinities and the History of Languages", is of itself a sufficient pledge for the permanent attention henceforth to be paid in England to linguistic studies. I may also here record the fact that three German names appear among the contributors to the last number, and several more on the list of members.

CHAPTER III.

Selbst in der Künste Heiligthum zu steigen,
Hat sich der deutsche Genius erkühnt,
Und auf der Spur des Griechen und des Britten
Ist er dem bessern Ruhme nachgeschritten.

Schiller.

THE ENGLISH LANGUAGE CONSIDERED FROM A LITERARY POINT OF VIEW.

The English having, in the preceding chapter, been proved to be a Germanic language, it follows as a natural result, that its literature must bear a close affinity to our own, and I will, therefore, now endeavour to show that, for three reasons, English Literature has peculiar and pre-eminent claims to the attention of the German student. They are, 1. The affinity it bears to our own; 2. The mutual influence the two literatures have exercised on each other at different periods, and 3. The high intrinsic merit of English Literature itself. In order to establish the first position, I need but remind the reader that the language and literature of a people necessarily stand in the closest connexion with each other. However mighty and original an author's genius, he cannot escape the natural influence of the language — the instrument of his thoughts — which will under all circumstances direct them. Both the individual and the nation at large are in this respect subject to that law of reciprocal action which I alluded to in the preceding chapter. And, as in the language of a people its characteristics may be traced, so also, and more distinctly, in its literature, which is the emanation of those minds that have enjoyed a superior culture, and are the true exponents of the national character. This remark applies more especially to the poets of a country: for it is in their effusions that we are best enabled to trace the distinguishing peculiarities of a nation's intellectual endowments. Science has a universal, poetry alone a special or national character. We all reason alike, but we feel differently. We are all, it is true, subject to the same passions, but our feelings are modified by circumstances, and it is only so far as these feelings affect the mind that the train of thought, too, in different nations, varies. — In the poetry of a nation its mode of thinking, as modified and influenced by the feelings, finds its truest expression, and tho these, therefore, we must resort, if we wish to study the characteristics of a nation. Now, in English literature, by which I would be understood to refer to the works just indicated, we discover, as in the language, a spirit akin to that pervading our own literature, and, instead of all elaborate argument, it will suffice to point to the highest instance, to Shakspeare — the poet who, above all others, stands most prominently forward as the exponent and representative of the national mind, and whom we have succeeded in making almost entirely our own. So much has been written on the influence of that unrivalled poet on our own literature, and on the gradually growing appreciation of his merits in our country, that it is needless for me here to dwell upon these facts at any great length. The curious reader will meet ample literary notices on the subject in the works of Horn [1] and Koberstein [2], while the bibliographer will find his curiosity satisfied in the useful little volume of Sillig,[3] on the Shakspeare Literature. But I have before me an able and interesting treatise, entitled, "Shakspeare in

---

[1] "Shakspeare's Schauspiele, erläutert von Franz Horn." Leipzig 1823. vol. I. Einleitung.

[2] "Historische Skizze über das allmälige Bekanntwerden Shakspeare's in Deutschland und die Meinungen über ihn bis 1773." Von Dr. A. Koberstein. Leipzig, Barth, 1850. Compare also Adolph Stahr's "Shakspeare in Deutschland", in Prutz's lit.-hist. Taschenbuch 1843.

[3] "Die Shakspeare-Literatur bis 1854, zusammengestellt und herausgegeben von P. H. Sillig." Leipzig, Dyk'sche Buchhandlung, 1854.

Germany"[4], from which I will extract one or two passages. — Having quoted a statement of Tieck's[5], on the subject of the English Comedians who, at the beginning of the 17. Century, visited Germany and particularly Dresden, where they principally performed pieces copied from those of Shakspeare's contemporaries or immediate predecessors, and even by himself — Titus Andronicus having been so exhibited —, the writer, who has availed himself of all the German sources within his reach, proceeds to say, "This intimacy with England and its drama appears to have suddenly and entirely ceased, at the precise time when it might have been most advantageous to Germany; and German poetry of all kinds, from the period of its first national poets and the Minnesingers, gradually submitted to the domination of French taste, and acknowledged the system and the laws which it prescribed. Soon after the commencement of the eighteenth century, however, German poetry began to show symptoms of reviving independence, though the first impulse came from without."

"J. J. Bodmer, a native of Zurich, felt and lamented the want of distinctive character in the literature of his native language, which, formed in

---

[4] See "The Complete Works of Shakspeare. Baudry's Ed. Paris 1844." vol. IX. p. 351.

[5] From Tieck's Einleitung zum Altenglischen Theater.

the school of Gottsched, Gellert, and Weisse, followed slavishly and heavily in the footsteps of its French models. Bodmer, a thorough Greek and Latin as well as English scholar, made an attack on this school in 1728 in his 'Anklage wegen des verderbten Geschmacks' ('Denouncement of Depraved Taste'), and he was ably seconded in other critical works by his friend Breitinger. Gottsched, then the predominating literary authority, opposed the new principles of criticism with extreme violence and considerable skill, and, supported by his adherents, a war of pamphlets and journals raged for years. But Bodmer had recourse to stronger weapons than critical arguments. He translated Homer and Milton into German[6], and published a collection of the old romantic ballads of Germany. His doctrines triumphed, though slowly; and *all the subsequent writers of any eminence* were more or less influenced by his opinions. These controversies inevitably led the attention of literary men back again to England and Shakspeare, as it was thence that the opponents of the French style drew some of the strongest supports

[6] Gervinus, speaking of Bodmer's translation of Milton, uses these words, "This is an astonishingly important act in the history of our literature." See his "Neuere Geschichte der poet. National-Literatur der Deutschen." 1. Theil. Leipzig 1840, also under the title of "Geschichte der deutschen Dichtung", vol. IV. p. 56. (*Author's Note.*)

for their new theories; and there has probably never been an instance in which a foreign author has been so completely adopted into, and had so much influence upon, the national literature of a country, as in the case of Shakspeare in Germany. Although scarcely known for a long period after his death, and even then principally through the French, his power and magnificence seem at once to have been felt and acknowledged, though his high dramatic art and extreme correctness of characterization were not always at first fully comprehended." Even Wieland, who had the strongest leaning to French taste, was finally won over to the other side by the criticisms of Lessing, and by his own study of English literature. Of our great classics, Herder was the next who sided with Lessing[7] in favour of Shakspeare and against the

[7] What Lessing, the two Schlegels, and Tieck have done for Shakspeare is too well known for me here to dilate upon. As regards England's great poet, Germany indeed may be said to have made a good return for the benefits received. Nor have English critics been slow to acknowledge the great merit of their German brethren and fellow-labourers. "It was Lessing", said Coleridge, "who first proved to all thinking men — even to Shakspeare's countrymen — the true nature of his apparent irregularities." (See 'Biogr. Literaria', vol. II. p. 256.) A. W. Schlegel's Lectures have been translated into English by Dr. Black, and English commentators have largely availed themselves of the valuable criticisms of that writer, who, conjointly with Tieck, has furnished us with a trans-

French tragedians, and he it was who made the Germans acquainted with Percy's "Reliques of Ancient Poetry", which, as Gervinus says, gave an extraordinary impulse to Germany. In these ancient Reliques Herder traced a strong resemblance between English and German Poetry of the middle ages, and thus, another proof in favour of the congeniality of these two nations in literary taste was established. Herder, in his turn, led Goethe to the study of Shakspeare and Ossian, and taught him to appreciate the "Vicar of Wakefield", that charming novel, equally popular in Germany and in England, and of which W. A. Schlegel has said, "Of all novels in miniature (and this I hold to be the best shape for novels to appear in), I think 'the Vicar of Wakefield' the most exquisite." — "It is not easy for us", says Lewes[8] with reference to Shakspeare,

---

lation that stands unrivalled in the history of literature, and takes a high rank as a classical work in our own language. Nor can we omit here the names of Ulrici, Gervinus, Mommsen, Kreyssig, and Delius, who, in more recent times, have continued the labors of their predecessors, and have contributed, either by aesthetical or exegetical commentaries, their share in elucidating the great British poet. — The last most note-worthy addition made to the Shaksp. Lit. in Germany is Tycho Mommsen's "Crit. Ed. of Romeo and Julia etc. etc. Oldenburg, G. Stalling, 1859."

[8] See "The Life and Works of Goethe etc. by G. H. Lewes." 2. Edit. vol. I. Leipzig, F. A. Brockhaus, 1858. p. 113. The "Oration on Shakspeare", delivered by Goethe

"to imagine the effect which the revelation of such a mind as this must have produced on the young Germans. The colossal strength, the profundity of thought, the originality and audacity of language, the brevity, pathos, sublimity, wit, and wild overflowing humour, the free movement of life, and the accuracy of observation as well as depth of insight into the mysteries of passion and character, were qualities which no false criticism, and, above all, no national taste, prevented Germans from appreciating" . . . "To the Germans, Shakspeare was a standard borne by all who combated against France, and his greatness was recognized with something of wilful preference. The state of German literature also rendered his influence the more prodigious." As to Schiller, he confesses to having required a long time ere he could comprehend this individuality. "I was not yet fit", he adds, "to comprehend nature at first hand."[9] Nevertheless, it is he who has given us a translation of Macbeth, and who finally became even a more enthusiastic admirer of Shakspeare than Goethe himself. "Had Schiller lived longer", says Gervinus, "he would perhaps have done more for the introduction of

---

at a meeting of the Shakspeare-Circle, is also published here for the first time, the biographer being indebted to Otto Jahn for this highly interesting document.

[9] See "Lewes, as above", p. 119.

Shakspeare on the German stage than Goethe, and with a more sincere love." This, by the way, is quite a characteristic feature of our Schiller's mental constitution as contrasted with Goethe's. "To the former", to use Carlyle's language, "nothing came without a strenuous effort; the latter seized all at one grasp of his capacious mind"; the former, to use still more famous and pithy language, "achieved greatness, the latter was born great." On the other hand, Goethe, by virtue of that grace divine with which he was endowed, was more subject to fits and starts, was more the creature of impulse than the less gifted, yet more ardent and persevering Schiller. Goethe's genius may be likened to the sudden bright blaze that illumines; Schiller's, to the genial, tho' slow fire that warms. To return, however, from this digression. On reviewing the history of modern German literature, we find that the influence which English literature exercised on it was by no means confined to Shakspeare alone. Bodmer's translation of Milton has already been mentioned.[10] His was the period (1698—1783) of the dawning of an improved taste, and, in conjunction with Breitinger, Liscow, and others, most of whom were, equally with him, great admirers of, and had deeply studied, English literature, he

---

[10] A second translation by Zachariae appeared at Altona, in 1760.

formed what is known in literary history by the appellation of the Swiss or Zurich school, constituting a stout opposition to Gottsched, the advocate of French taste. As early as 1719 Bodmer had become acquainted with Addison's Spectator, and, associating with Breitinger and others, he copied that model, and published with them the "Discourses of Painters" (1721—22). Waser, whom Gervinus describes as being of a Swiftian character, translated (1756) that great satirist. Luise Gottsched, about the same time, translated Addison's "Cato" and Pope's "Rape of the Lock." Rabener (1714—1771) was an imitator, tho' but a poor one, of Swift. Ebert (1723—1795) so successfully translated Young's "Night Thoughts", that the author paid him the high compliment of declaring that the translation was an improvement upon the original. These "Night Thoughts" were indeed of no small effect on the German mind. The influence of Milton on Klopstock requires but a passing mention. Thomson's "Seasons" probably led to Kleist's "Spring." Uz (1720—96) imitated Pope. Michael Denis (1729—1800) is chiefly celebrated as the translator of Ossian. J. P. Hermes (1738—1821) imitated Richardson. As the earliest translators of one or more Dramas of Shakspeare I have to name Wieland, Eschenbach, Weisse, and Bürger. The latter, like Herder before him, by felicitous adaptations, transplanted Scotch ballad-poetry on the

German soil. Hippel, Musaeus, Thümmel, and others wrote and conducted themselves on the model of the English Humourists, especially on that of Sterne, who, at a subsequent period, found another and more successful imitator in J. Paul Richter. The great historians, Hume, Robertson, and Gibbon, soon met with their translators. The latter, in his Memoirs, after estimating, at their respective value, the French and Italian versions of his great work, adds, "But I wish it were in my power to read the German, which is praised by the best judges." Leibnitz, Mendelssohn, and his illustrious friend Lessing were enthusiastic admirers of Shaftesbury. But, above all, it was Locke whom the two friends most assiduously studied, and from whose writings they drew their principal nourishment. Nor were Hobbes, or Berkeley, or Newton, or Adam Smith neglected by German scholars. But the influence of all these philosophers dwindles down almost to nothing, when we come to Hume, for his is the great merit of having given the impulse to Kant, who was candid enough to acquaint the world with the fact. "I freely confess", says he in his Prolegomena, "it was the memory of David Hume which, many years ago, for the first time broke my dogmatical slumber, and gave my investigations in the field of speculative philosophy quite a different direction." Surely I need not, after this, proceed in my enumeration of English authors whose writings have exercised any influence on German literature. It is true, Germany has by far outstripped England in the boldness of her speculations; but, after this acknowledgment on the part of Kant, it would be vain for us, his posterity, to deny the sister country the merit of having influenced our great philosopher, the teacher of Schiller, and the father of our modern philosophy.

It has, hitherto, been my object to show, in the merest outlines, how, from the dawning of our second period of classical literature up to its culmination in Goethe and Schiller, the minds of all our great writers were tinctured by, and saturated with, the literature and speculative theories of the British isles[11]: it will now be my task to show how, from that period, a reciprocity of influence took its date; how an interchange, as it were, of ideas commenced to take place between the two kindred nations, and continued to be carried on, Germany finally predominating, and, making ample returns for what she had originally received, in her turn influencing English literature, and, from a

---

[11] I use this term here advisedly, as it includes Ireland, Scotland, and Wales — the countries of a Moore, a Scott, an Ossian or a Macpherson (it matters not now which), a Burns, and other poets not unknown to fame, as well as of many of the ballads that became popular in Germany, tho', I trust, I shall be excused for classing the productions of all these countries under the head of English literature.

state of pupillage, rising to become the teacher. Gervinus, who dates the opposite tendencies of the northern, Protestant or Germanic, to those of the southern, Catholic or Romance nations from the time when Bacon attacked scholastic philosophy, and Shakspeare abandoned the Italian taste, may fitly be cited here in support both of what has preceded, and of what I have yet to bring forward. "At the time when Shakspeare first gave the impulse", he says, "there was too little intellectual communication and interchange of language in the world, and England was too remote and even too small a country for the Germanic intellectual tendencies to have, then and thence, been diffused, and obtained any dominion over the literatures of Europe; but now, when in Germany these very tendencies, in closest approximation to English literature, had been resumed in the centre of this part of the world, and from a populous country whose language and tribes extended to all the frontier land; at a time when the widest communication facilitated the intellectual intercourse of all nations, the moment had arrived, when that peculiar character of Germanic literature spread in all directions, and, German literature especially, having attained the highest degree of cultivation, established simultaneously with, and, as it were, in emulation of, the political ascendancy of France, a universal dominion of mind, more durable, and of no less historical importance."[12] To mark the precise period at which the reaction of Germany on England commenced, I must be allowed to quote another passage from the same historian. After cursorily mentioning Ossian, Percy's Reliques, W. Scott's collection of the Minstrelsy of the Scottish Border, Robert Burns, the farmer's son, Hogg, the Ettrick shepherd boy, and Allan Cunningham, the mason, he proceeds to say, "This revived poetry of nature and the people" (as contrasted with the artificial and court poetry of the Restoration, pervaded by French taste,) "had acted on Germany, where, soon after, it produced a reaction." Bürger's two ballads, "Lenore" and "the Wild Hunter", having been translated (1794—96) respectively by Taylor and Scott, attracted, in Edinburgh, the attention of Scott's circle of friends wholly to German literature. In ballad-poetry Scott, Lewis, Coleridge, Wordsworth, and others first followed in the wake of the Germans, and, tracing their steps backward from Bürger to Wieland, they advanced to the amplified epic narrative, which borrowed its matter from the romantic middle-ages. In this species Walter Scott earned for himself, in his first poetical period (1805), the appellation of a modern Ariosto." Gervinus, however, is inclined to ascribe

---

[12] See "Geschichte des 19. Jahrhunderts seit den Wiener Verträgen, von G. G. Gervinus." vol. I. Leipzig 1855. p. 402.

to him rather an external than any great internal influence on German literature, tho', in his History of the Poetical Literature of Germany, he allows him to have indirectly called forth among us an improved class of the historical novel, and Bronikowsky, Häring, Spindler, Zschokke, Tieck, and others are named as his successors in that species of literature.[13] Julian Schmidt goes farther and concedes to him, in addition, a most salutary influence on the manner of treating history. "That our modern historians", he says, "endeavour to measure every age by its own standard, to regard every historical character as a work of art in itself, and to reproduce, in vivid imitation, the local colour of the scene where the action is laid, instead of diluting it by smooth reasoning, having merely the semblance of narrative, is mainly owing to his influence."[14] As to Lord Byron, it is well known that he and Goethe were great admirers of each other, and, without being a German scholar himself, the British bard owned himself indebted to German literature, and more especially to Goethe's productions, while he, in his turn, subsequently

---

[13] See "Neuere Geschichte der poetischen Nationalliteratur der Deutschen", vol. V. p. 696.

[14] See "Geschichte der classischen Nationalliteratur des 19. Jahrhunderts, von J. Schmidt." First Edition. Leipzig. vol. I. p. 37.

reacted on German literature, favouring and fostering that subjectivism which had, indeed, already found so strong an expression in Werther, but which, in the course of Goethe's literary activity, had given way to the objective character of his more finished and classical works. It will, I hope, not be uninteresting to my readers to meet here with a few details, serving to set in a clear light Byron's connection with German literature.[15] In June 1820, Lord Byron thus writes to his publisher Mr. Murray. "Enclosed is something which will interest you, to wit, the opinion of the greatest man in Germany — perhaps in Europe — upon one of the great men of your advertisements — in short, a critique upon *Manfred*. There is the original, an English translation, and an Italian one: keep them all in your archives; for the opinions of such a man as Goethe, whether favourable or not, are always interesting — and this is more so as favourable. His Faust I never read, for I don't know German, but Mathew Monk Lewis, in 1816, at Coligny, translated most of it to me vivâ voce, and I was naturally much struck with it; .....

---

[15] For observations of Goethe concerning Byron, I can do no better than refer the reader to Eckermann's "Dialogues with Goethe", where he will find them profusely interspersed throughout the work.

The first scene, and that of Faustus are very similar[16].

The following is an extract from Goethe's critique, as published in "Kunst und Alterthum", and referred to in the above letter. "Byron's tragedy, 'Manfred', was to me a wonderful phenomenon, and one that closely touched me. This singularly intellectual poet has taken my Faustus to himself, and extracted from it the strongest nourishment for his hypochondriac humour. He has made use of the impelling principles in his own way, for his own purposes, so that no one of them remains the same, and it is particularly on this account that I cannot enough admire his genius." Besides intending to dedicate his "Marino Faliero" to Goethe[17], he did inscribe to him his "Sardanapalus" (1821) in these terms, "To the illustrious Goethe a stranger presumes to offer the homage of a literary vassal

---

[16] See Note to "Manfred", in Byron's "Works, Complete in One Volume." London, J. Murray, 1846. p. 191. The opening lines of the 'Bride of Abydos', "Know ye the land, where the cypress and myrtle" &c. are also supposed to have been suggested by Goethe's "Kennst du das Land, wo die Citronen blühen." (ibidem, p. 77)

[17] "His letter to that effect did not reach the hands of Goethe till 1835, when it was presented to him at Weimar, by Mr. Murray jun., nor was it printed at all, until Thomas Moore included it in his Life of Lord Byron." (See Byron's "Works", as above, p. 197).

to his liege-lord, the first of existing writers, who has created the literature of his own country, and illustrated that of Europe!" Whereupon Goethe remarks, "Well knowing myself and my labours, in my old age, I could not but reflect with gratitude and diffidence on the expressions contained in this dedication, nor interpret them but as the generous tribute of a superior genius, no less original in the choice than inexhaustible in the material of his subjects." [18] Here, then, we have arrived at the turning point of the literary history of both countries, as represented in their two greatest poets of modern times. Goethe, nourished at the breasts of English literature, is held in the highest veneration, and sometimes imitated by Byron, while the English bard, in his turn, eulogized and admired by Goethe, reacts on German, nay, indeed, on European literature. For it was he who, together with Lamartine, Chateaubriand, and Victor Hugo in France, continued, and disseminated over Europe, that poetry of "distraction" and "world-woe", to which, as stated before, the cue had been given by the "Sorrows of Werther", a work of which an early translation appeared in English. In fact, he

---

[18] Letter 523 in Byron's Life, by Thomas Moore, contains another tribute of Goethe's to Byron's genius; but I think the lines unworthy of our great poet, or, at least, not sufficiently characteristic of him to quote them.

was "the greatest of romanticists", as Shaw [19] styles him, and, so far at least, notwithstanding his reiterated admiration of the classical, yet artificial Pope, Byron was involuntarily and despite of himself, as it were, a follower of Shakspeare rather than of the poetry of Queen Anne's reign.

But we now come to another school of poets, who had more largely than he drawn at the fountain of German literature, and caught its spirit. It is the so-called "Lake School", headed by Wordsworth. Craik,[20] in his introductory remarks on the literature of the nineteenth century, defining the three periods into which English literature is commonly divided, says, "It is also to be observed that on each of these three occasions the excitement appears to have come to us in part from a foreign literature which had undergone a similar re-awakening or put forth a new life and vigor, shortly before our own: in the Elizabethan age the contagion or impulse was caught from the literature of Italy; in the age of Queen Anne from that of France; in the present period from that of Germany." — "This German inspiration", continues our author, "operated most directly, and produced the

---

[19] See "Outlines of English Literature" by T. B. Shaw. London 1849, p. 432.

[20] See "His Sketches of the History of Literature and Learning in England." Ser. III. vol. VI. p. 113.

most marked effect, in the poetry of Wordsworth." That poet[21] had, as early as 1798, accompanied by his friend S. T. Coleridge, visited Germany for the purpose of acquiring a thorough knowledge of the German language, literature, and philosophy. Coleridge soon after produced a successful translation of "Wallenstein", and, thenceforth, English literature caught more and more of the spirit of German literature, and soon visibly manifested the impulse thence received. No one, however, had a greater share in introducing German literature into England, and in promoting a more extensive acquaintance with it among his own countrymen than Thomas Carlyle[22]. Nor is there any living author in England whose writings have more powerfully influenced, and given a more decided bent to, the

---

[21] For a characterisation of his poetry, I must refer the reader to Shaw's „Outlines" p. 518, or to my own "England's Dichter und Prosaisten der Neuzeit", being the fourth volume of "Ideler and Nolte's Handbuch der Englischen Sprache und Literatur." Berlin 1853. A. Nauck, and London, D. Nutt. Introduction p. XV, where the above passage from Shaw is also quoted in German.

[22] Foremost among those who, shortly after, followed in his footsteps, I have to mention Mrs. Sarah Austin, "who, as an interpreter between the mind of Germany and the mind of Britain (I am quoting Macaulay's words), has already deserved so well of both countries." For more copious information on this subject, see an able article, from the pen of Herm. Marggraff, headed "Deutsche Literatur, Wissenschaft u. Kunst im Ausl.", in Brockhaus' Gegenwart, part. 139. p. 261—281.

poets of the present day than that great Scotch thinker whose mind is so deeply imbued with the doctrines of German philosophy. The Brownings, A. Tennyson, the Hon. Mrs. Norton, B. Disraeli (in his Sibyl), Ch. Kingsley[23], and a host of others, tacitly at least, acknowledge his influence, and rank among his disciples, whose number also includes Lewes, the author of "the Life of Goethe", a work which may be said to cement on the part of the English the bonds of intellectual affinity that unite the two nations, and makes Goethe as much the common property of both as Shakspeare has long become so through the translations and commentaries of the Germans.

Bulwer, grateful for the benefit he derived from the study of German literature and philosophy, dedicated his "Ernest Maltravers" to the German nation, and, at a later period of his literary activity, translated Schiller's poems, thus adding another stone to the "heap to be a witness" between the two nations of their close mental alliance and congenial tastes. On the other hand, where has that brilliant novelist, just named, — where have the no less powerful Dickens and Thackeray — where have a Marryat and a Lever, and other English writers of fiction, too numerous to men-

[23] For particulars about these authors and their connexion with Carlyle, see my work as quoted above.

tion found more admiring readers than in Germany? The success of the Tauchnitz edition of their works would alone suffice to remove any doubt on the subject. Indeed, the "Collection of British Authors", from Shakspeare to Dickens' "Household Words", has become a household property in Germany, and every new work of fiction, sent forth by the English press, is looked forward to and devoured with as much avidity here as in England. Nor is the love of English literature confined only to those who possess the language: but numerous translations speedily render the most popular English authors accessible to the general public, and the reader of the German version chuckles almost as heartliy over the broad humour of a "Pickwick" and the witty sallies of a "Sam Weller", and enjoys, as intensely as any English reader, the scheming and subtlety of a "Becky Sharp." — Again, to ascend to a higher species of literature, of Macaulay's History of England, tho' a decidedly national work, we have almost as many translations as of Shakspeare, and his brilliant "Essays" find as much favour with the German public as with the English. Thus there is, between the English and the Germans, a reciprocal giving and taking, a mutual interchange of ideas, such as is nowhere else to be met with. And it is worthy of note that as, in the individual instance of Shakspeare, we have made an ample return for what we have received, so German literature[24] on the whole, having first received the impulse from England, in its turn influenced English literature, and no one can be said to have a thorough knowledge of either who is not acquainted with both. As to the third reason which I assigned at the commencement of this chapter in assertion of the claims of English literature, viz, its high instrinsic merit, I feel, so much has been said on that head in this Essay that it would be a work of supererogation on my part here to dwell upon this topic again at any length. The great names I have mentioned, shining forth pre-eminent in the multifarious walks of literature—as historians, philosophers, and orators — as dramatic, epic, and lyric poets — as novelists and humorists — are a sufficient guarantee for the sterling merit of the works constituting English literature, and the acquaintance of my readers with the majority of them, which, I believe, I may unhesitatingly presume on, dispenses me from all elaborate argument. Nor is there any necessity to point out the great advantage which the so-called light literature offers, both to parents and teachers, in educational respects: for the high moral tone of English society, acting

---

[24] I need scarcely remark that, in speaking of German literature, I would be always understood to refer to our second classical period, our first being entirely original and purely national.

as it does as a wholesome check on authors of a depraved taste, and rendering it impossible for an immoral book to stand, is too well known to require being dilated upon by me, and the reading public has long since discovered that a mother may place almost any English novel in the hands of her daughter, and that a teacher may read almost any light work with his pupils, without having to entertain any fears on the score of morality. Whether, therefore, we view English literature by itself, excelling as it does in almost all branches, unsurpassed as it is in some, and immaculately pure as are even its lightest productions; or whether we regard it as connected with our own, mutually elucidating and bearing upon each other as they have been shown to do, the language which has given birth to that literature, and in which it is conveyed, deserves the highest claims on our attention, and must be of paramount importance to all who aspire to rank among the educated classes of society.

CHAPTER IV

> Go forth, and jointly speed the time,
> By good men prayed for long.
> When Christian states, grown just and wise,
> Will scorn revenge and wrong;
> When earth's oppressed and savage tribes
> Shall cease to pine or roam,
> All taught to prize these England's words —
> Faith, Freedom, Heaven and Home.
>
> J. G. Lyons (ut supra).

THE ENGLISH LANGUAGE CONSIDERED FROM A PRACTICAL POINT OF VIEW.

Lastly, then, I purpose to consider the English language from a practical point of view, or, to state it in plain terms, to enquire, how far the utilitarian, that is, he who, before entering on any pursuit, asks the matter-of-fact question "cui bono"? and is not to be moved until he has satisfied his own mind that there are substantial advantages to be derived from the pursuit — in short, how far the practical man, the merchant or trader who leaves scientific investigation to the learned, and thinks, and in many respects justly so, that he finds in the literature of his own country sufficient nourishment for his mind, can be benefited by studying the English language. There was a time, and it is not very remote, when the French was actually the universal language or, at least, bade fair to assume that character; when it was as indispensable for the courtier as for the valet, for the commercial traveller as for the man of letters, to be able to converse in the language of Voltaire and Rousseau. But even in their age the English language, tho', to all outward appearance, outshone by the French, had commenced to acquire a more extensive dominion, and to make rapid strides towards a more general diffusion. As early as 1767, David Hume, the celebrated philosopher and historian, having received a MS. copy of Gibbon's "Historical Essay upon the Liberty of the Swiss" (which was never published), wrote to the author in the following terms[1], "Sir, — It is but a few days ago since Mr. Deyverdun put your manuscript into my hands, and I have perused it with great pleasure and satisfaction. I have only one objection, derived from the language in which it is written. Why do you compose in French, and carry faggots into the wood, as Horace says with regard to Romans who wrote in Greek? I grant that you have a like motive to those Romans, and

[1] See "The Miscellaneous Works of E. Gibbon Esq. Edited by John, Lord Sheffield." London, B. Blake. 1857. p. 85. Note.

adopt a language much more generally diffused than your native tongue, but have you not remarked the fate of those two ancient languages in following ages? The Latin, tho' then less celebrated, and confined to more narrow limits, has in some measure outlived the Greek, and is now more generally understood by men of letters. Let the French, therefore, triumph in the present diffusion of their tongue. Our solid and increasing establishment in America, where we need less dread the inundation of barbarians, promise a superior stability and duration to the English language.". — "Every year that has since elapsed", hereupon remarks. Mr. Watts, in a valuable paper on "the Probable Future Position of the English Language"[2], has added a superior degree of probability to the anticipation of Hume. At present the prospects of the English language are the most splendid that the world has ever seen. It is spreading in each of the quarters of the globe by fashion, by emigration, and by conquest. The increase of population alone in the two great States of Europe and America in which it is spoken, adds to the number of its speakers in every year that passes, a greater amount than the whole number of those who speak some of the lite-

---

[2] In the "Transactions of the Philological Society, No. 92." Compare also Latham, "The English Language", p. 566—572, from whence I quote.

rary languages of Europe, either Swedish, or Danish, or Dutch. It is calculated that, before the lapse of the present century, a time that so many now alive will live to witness, it will be the native and vernacular language of about one hundred and fifty millions of human beings."

"What will be the state of Christendom at the time that this vast preponderance of one language will be brought to bear on all its relations, — at the time when a leading nation in Europe and a gigantic nation in America make use of the same idiom, when in Africa and Australasia the same language is in use by rising and influential communities, and the world is circled by the accents of Shakspeare and Milton? At that time such of the other languages of Europe as do not extend their empire beyond this quarter of the globe will be reduced to the same degree of insignificance in comparison with English, as the subordinate languages of modern Europe to those of the state they belong to, — the Welsh to the English, the Basque to the Spanish, the Finnish to the Russian. This predominance, we may flatter ourselves, will be a more signal blessing to literature than that of any other language could possibly be. The English is essentially a medium language; in the Teutonic family it stands midway between the Germanic and Scandinavian branches — it unites, as no other language unites, the Romanic and Teutonic stocks.

This fits it admirably in many cases for translation."[3] But here I must stop in my quotation, my object in this chapter being, to consider the English language from a practical or social, not from a literary point of view. In that respect, we need no longer dwell on, or point out in glowing colours, its glorious prospect, but simply cast a glance at the map of the world, to survey the actual extent of the language. Besides predominating in the Western world, it has travelled, with the nomadic natives of the British isles, into their Asiatic dominions, stretching from the Indus to the Ganges; has established itself in the islands of the Indian ocean, and on the Chinese coasts; over the whole face of our Antipodes, and on the Western and Southern extremities of Africa; has planted its foot on the Spanish Rock, and seized on the Ionian isles, so that from the rise of the sun, aye, unto the setting thereof — the uttermost western boundaries of the new world, its accents may be heard, tho' intermingled with other tongues that help to enrich it with new words, and contribute to enlarge its vocabulary[4]. Wherever, then, the merchant turns his eye with a view to extend his

---

[3] Compare also Trench, "Engl. Past and Present", p. 35.

[4] I trust, the qualification appended to the sentence will suffice to atone for the rather hyperbolical language into which I have allowed myself to be hurried by my enthusiasm.

commercial transactions, English will be found the most convenient medium of communication: for in almost every corner of the globe he will meet with either an English colony, or factory, or station, or, at least, scattered residents engaged in commerce, ready to facilitate his projects, and to aid him in his mercantile speculations. Indeed, I may venture to maintain that English is now as indispensable to the merchant as French still is to the man of fashion and to the diplomatist, and that his education is imperfect without a knowledge of a language spoken by the two greatest commercial nations of the world.

Nor can the manufacturer, or the agriculturist, or the engineer, or any one engaged in mechanical or technical pursuits of any kind dispense with that knowledge, if he would with advantage carry on his labours: for in all these branches English periodicals abound in information eminently calculated to promote his progress. The numerous technical terms, too, derived from the English language are a sufficient evidence of the start which England, in these branches, has of other countries, and hence, a scientific treatise, even in German, must remain partially unintelligible to him who is unacquainted with English. Whether, therefore, we regard that language from a linguistic, or literary, or practical point of view, I trust, I have not altogether failed in showing that it possesses the highest claims on our attention, and deserves to occupy a prominent rank in any system of education that aspires to be styled complete.

In conclusion, I shall briefly point out on what plan the study of the language should be pursued in a commercial school. The course is already indicated in what has preceded. Unintentionally, my investigation of the subject has led to this final result, so that my practical hints will be found to coincide with my theoretical enquiry. Supposing, then, a school to consist of three classes (which is the case in the commercial academy of Leipsic), and the rudiments of the language to have been previously acquired by the pupils, we shall, in the first year, have to ground them more thoroughly in the Grammar, and to enrich their memory with a treasure of words, the "*sine quâ non*" for the purposes of conversation and reading. Etymological analyses, or parsing, aided by comparative philology, will have to accompany the exercises in translation, and the most vigilant attention should be bestowed on correct pronunciation, which, being neglected in the first period, can never after be acquired. Any faults contracted at the beginning will always adhere, and cannot again be eradicated. Hence, too, the teacher should address himself chiefly to the ear of the pupil, and train that organ for the due reception of the sounds, the only efficient method of enabling him accurately to reproduce them. The organs of speech, too, will have to be carefully watched, and any vicious habits contracted by the pupil in the articulation and enunciation of his words corrected and obviated.

A good foundation having thus been laid, in the second class the student will have to be introduced into the literature, for which purpose a good anthology will have to be used, containing select pieces from the best authors, both in prose and poetry, accompanied by sketches of their lives and writings. The Syntax will also have to be proceeded with; the ear will have to be practised by writing from dictation, by interrogation on the subjects read, and oral translation from English into German and vice versâ, both from sight and hearing. Lastly, in the third year, the principal object of the teacher should be, to enable the student to express himself with ease and fluency, as well as correctly and idiomatically, both in conversation and in writing, cultivating especially the epistolary style, and more particularly the commercial style of correspondence with its peculiar and stereotyped phraseology, without, however, neglecting the literature. On the contrary, as far as time permits, the teacher should now pursue it on a more systematic plan, and impart to the student a general knowledge of the history of literature, always having regard to the more eminent authors, or such as have struck out for themselves new paths, and become the founders of new schools. It is to be expected ,that the pupil, guided by an intelligent teacher, and having, moreover, by this time made sufficient progress to read any author with ease, and without a too frequent recurrence to the dictionary, will feel interested in the literature of the language he has been studying, and be desirous of a more thorough acquaintance with its most valuable treasures. These, therefore, should be unlocked to him, or, the key being already in his possession, need but be pointed out to be eagerly resorted to by the inquisitive and diligent pupil. When, at a later period of his life, he shall be immersed in the turmoil, the stir, and the strife of this busy scene, he will be grateful to the teacher for having opened up to him higher sources of delight and enjoyment, and enabled him to partake of so rich an intellectual banquet, "the feast of reason and the flow of soul", hospitably spread out for all comers, a truly royal banquet, where the viands are prepared by kings and princes themselves, where the beverage is equally pure and high-flavoured, and such as "cheers, but does not inebriate." And such should be the final aim of linguistic as well of all other studies: the highest end of man should ever be held in view, particularly in the palmy, or rather holy, days of youth, where no immediate necessity gives the impulse, or exercises stern command, and where, therefore, all the faculties of the mind should be allowed to have ample scope, and to range freely over the unbounded fields of knowledge. To study a language merely for practical purposes is a pursuit unworthy of youth; to study it only for philological reasons is the business of the scholar; but in every station of life the possession of so useful a key cannot but be a valuable acquisition, and certainly not least so to the merchant who, destined as he is to be the bearer of civilisation to remote climes, and mixing as he does with the intelligent classes of various countries, besides affording no small delight to others, will derive no less satisfaction to himself from an acquaintance with the literary treasures of the country he may happen to visit: he will then stand forth a worthy representative of the intelligence of his own nation, and ensure respect for his countrymen in general and for himself individually.

SUPPLEMENTARY NOTES.

Page 6. Note 4.

After a further perusal of the bibliographical portion of Schmitz's Encyclopaedia I see no cause to retract any thing of what I have said in its commendation above: but I cannot forbear expressing my regret that the author should have exhibited so singular a want of filial reverence as to speak disparagingly, nay, even contemptuously, of his father's publications. Whatever may be their deficiencies, I humbly opine, the mere mention of the titles would have satisfied all the claims of the public and of science.

Page 6. Note 5.

The title of this Dictionary is, "Linguarum totius orbis vocabularia Augustissima (Catharinae II.) cura collecta", and the name of the compiler, Pallas. Schmitz, in his Encycl., however, mentions several similar compilations of a still earlier date, those of the traveller Pigafetta being published as early as 1536. See Schmitz, p. 17.

Page 8—12.

This quotation from Schopenhauer will, doubless, far better than all I have said, help, in some measure, to counteract the injurious effect of an article, recently published in the Westminster Review (July 1859), under the heading of, "What knowledge is most worth having?" — I say injurious, because although the writer himself seems well aware of the existence of such a science as comparative philology, and may, for aught I know, be himself no mean cultivator of it, yet the article would seem to be written with a tendency to disparage linguistic studies in the eye of the reader. Such, at least, is the general impression one gathers from the perusal of the paper, though in justice to the able writer it must be stated, and a more attentive perusal shows, that, in truth, he had no such intention, seeing that he declaims only against the study of languages as ordinarily carried on, not as pursued by earnest students. In fact, had he not pleaded so much more strongly in favour of the more practical sciences, he might be regarded as an advocate of, rather than as an opponent to, linguistic studies.

Page 17. Note 1.

All that is stated there refers to what may be termed the absolute euphony of the language. But there is also a relative euphony, depending on the individual speaker. On this head, Thackeray (The Virginians, vol. III. p. 287. Tauchn. Ed.) justly remarks, "All accents are pretty from pretty lips, and who shall set the standard up? And the great British poet, long before him, makes Mortimer say to his wife,

"Thy tongue
"Makes Welsh as sweet as ditties highly penn'd
"Sung by a fair queen in a summer's bower,
"With ravishing division, to her lute."
(Henry IV. P. I. Sc. I.)

Page 44. Note 39.

Besides the London Philol. Society, established in 1842, there are two others known to me for the special cultivation of Anglo-Saxon Literature, viz., the Aelfric and the Cambridge Antiquarian Society. Of the latter, I may mention here, for the benefit of my German readers whose notice it may have escaped, a publication, lying before me, by my friend Charles W. Goodwin Esq. M. A., containing "The Anglo-Saxon Legends of St. Andrew and St. Veronica, with an English Translation. Cambridge 1851."

Page 62.

By my placing the romantic poets of France in juxtaposition with Byron, the reader must, however, not be mis led to suppose that I have overlooked the essential difference between them and the English bard in a religions point of view.